THE
Little Book
— OF —
NATIVE
AMERICAN
WISDOM

In the same series

THE
Little Book
— OF —
NATIVE
AMERICAN
WISDOM

Compiled by
Steven McFadden

ISBN 1-84333-083-0

A catalogue record for this book is available
from the British Library

First published in 2002 by
Vega
64 Brewery Road
London, N7 9NT

A member of **Chrysalis** Books plc

Visit our website at www.chrysalisbooks.co.uk

Printed and bound in Thailand by Imago

Introduction

The true scope and depth of Native American wisdom is generally unknown, and much of what is known is misunderstood. This little book cannot hope to encompass the many levels of understanding that are part of Native American teachings, but it can hint at them, and it can strive to do so in a context appropriate for our times.

As we confront the complex problems of national and world cultures in transition, most people are looking for ways to move forward. While striving forward, we would do well to consider thoughtfully the voices that arise from Earth-based cultures, and to weave some of their enduring insights into the fabric of what we are creating for ourselves, our children, and our children's children. This would seem especially appropriate as, from 1995 to 2005, the world marks The United Nations' 'Decade of the World's Indigenous People'.

Native American peoples and cultures are as diverse as any other human community. There is no one point of view. The passages assembled here are but a representative sample. Still, the native peoples of America hold in common traditions of democracy and spiritual development that reach back tens of thousands of years. Further, Native American peoples agree that they have a specific spiritual responsibility as keepers of the Earth. This understanding can provide a helpful context for appreciating the history and relevance of Native wisdom.

Native wisdom is not just of the past, as some may mistakenly assume. In fact, some of the passages in this book are drawn from a historic presentation made by twenty-eight traditional Native American elders at the 'house of mica' – United Nations headquarters in New York City, on 22 November, 1993. The Cry of the Earth conference was an unprecedented gathering of world leaders with spiritual elders from all over North America, intended to focus attention on the ecological, spiritual, and ethical crises confronting humanity today. Sadly, not a word of their remarkable messages was reported at the time by the mass media.

The assembled teachings in this book call on us not to imitate or to try and become Native Americans, but rather to become the best human beings we can. The words of contemporary Native leaders, in particular, are tinged with a note of urgency. They share a sense that the time for profound change in human attitudes and behavior is short, and they encourage us to consider their voiced offerings promptly and carefully.

STEVEN MCFADDEN

They Will Return

MY FRIEND,

They will return again.
    All over the Earth,
They are returning again.
    Ancient teachings of the Earth,
Ancient songs of the Earth.
    They are returning again.
My friend, they are returning.
    I give them to you,
And through them
    You will understand,
You will see.
    They are returning again
Upon the Earth.

CRAZY HORSE,
Oglala Sioux (1842–77)

They Will Retrace Their Steps

THE SEVENTH PROPHET who came among the people long ago was different. He was young, and he had a strange look in his eye. He said, 'In the time of the Seventh Fire new people will emerge. They will retrace their steps to find what was left by the side of the trail long ago. Their steps will take them to the elders, who they will ask to guide them on their journey. But many of the elders will have fallen asleep. They will awaken to this new time with nothing to offer. Some of the elders will be silent out of fear. But most of the elders will be silent because no one will ask anything of them.'

TRADITIONAL CHIEF
WILLIAM COMMANDA,
Algonquin

Manitou

THE WORLD OF the Native American, spiritual and otherwise, is not to be understood by assuming that it can be described easily in the English language, and in religious terms. What we now think of as spirituality was not a religion in the commonly accepted definition of the word. It was their way of life, which is to say that it permeated their lives to such an extent as to be inseparable from everyday living . . . Manitou was not a supreme being, but rather a way of referring to the cosmic, mysterious power existing everywhere in nature.

EUNICE BAUMANN-NELSON, PH.D.,
Penobscot

In the Beginning

IN THE BEGINNING we were told that the human beings who walk about on the Earth have been provided with all of the things necessary for life. We were instructed to carry love for one another, and to show a great respect for all the beings of this Earth. We were shown that our well-being depends on the well-being of the vegetable life, and that we are close relatives of the four-legged beings.

HAUDENAUSENEE ELDERS,
Basic Call to Consciousness

Old and Proven Ideas

WISDOM DOES NOT belong to one person. We need to act in accord with wisdom, but it does not belong to anyone. It is the illumination of old and proven ideas through generation after generation of discovering natural law.

HUNBATZ MEN,
Daykeeper, Maya Nation

Our Elders Tell Us . . .

I FEEL PAIN AND ANGER that in your rush toward development, the fabric of this globe has been rent, and what you call the biosphere, or ecosphere — but which my people more simply call Mother — has been so neglected and hurt . . . . Our elders tell us we have to do more than save what is left of our traditional homelands. We need to contribute to an overall change of mind . . . so that human-kind can begin to initiate strategies which will preserve and sustain the environment that all cultures and nations share.

RUBY DUNSTAN,
Lytton Indian Band

To Walk In the Sacred Way

GRANDFATHER,
Look at our brokenness.

We know that in all Creation
Only the human family
Has strayed from the Sacred Way.

We know that we are the ones
Who are divided
And we are the ones
Who must come back together
To walk in the Sacred Way

Grandfather,
Sacred One,
Teach us love, compassion, honor
That we may heal the earth
And heal each other.

Ojibway Prayer

All Are Together

M IND OF SEPARATION, mind of domination, these have birthed genocide of Native peoples throughout the world: the Inquisition and the Nazi holocaust in Europe, the destruction of lands, cultures and peoples in Asia, and the invention of weaponry with power to kill all people on Earth twenty times over. In the Tsalagi teachings, such great sufferings are seen as unnecessary. They are the result of pride, the idea that one is better or more important than another. In reality, in the circle of right relationship, there is no above and no below, no in or out – all are together in the sacred circle.

DHYANI YWAHOO,
Etowah Band, Tsalagi (Cherokee)

So It Is In Everything

YOU HAVE NOTICED that everything an Indian does is in a circle, and that is because the Power of the World always works in circles, and everything tries to be round . . . . The sky is round, and I have heard that the earth is round like a ball, and so are all the stars. The wind, in its greatest power, whirls. Birds make their nests in circles, for theirs is the same religion as ours . . . . Even the seasons form a great circle in their changing, and always come back again to where they were. The life of a man is a circle from childhood to childhood, and so it is in everything where power moves.

BLACK ELK (1863-1950),
Oglala Sioux

Honor and Respect

To HONOR AND RESPECT means to think of the land and the water and plants and animals who live here as having a right equal to our own to be here. We are not the supreme and all-knowing beings, living at the top of the pinnacle of evolution, but in fact we are members of the sacred hoop of life, along with the trees and rocks, the coyotes and the eagles and fish and toads, that each fulfills its purpose. They each perform their given task in the sacred hoop, and we have one, too.

WOLF SONG,
Abenaki

Original Instructions

THE ORIGINAL INSTRUCTIONS are natural laws that were given to our people by the Creator, including the idea of respecting all things as part of the sacred circle of life. We are the generation with the responsibility and option to choose the path with a future for our children. We must join hands with the rest of creation, and speak of common sense responsibility, brotherhood, and peace.

OREN LYONS,
Faithkeeper, Onondaga Nation
10 December 1992 at UN Headquarters

Mending the Sacred Hoop

THE PROPHECIES of the ancestors of the Lakota Nations have important meaning for the future of Mother Earth. Through generations, these prophecies have been maintained courageously, methodically, and accurately. Now we are in a critical stage of our spiritual, moral and technological development as nations. All life is precariously balanced. We must remember that all things on Mother Earth have spirit and are intricately related. The Lakota prophecy of Mending the Sacred Hoop of all nations has begun. May we find, in the ancient wisdom of the Indigenous Nations, the spirit and courage to mend and heal.

ARVOL LOOKING HORSE,
Keeper of the Sacred Pipe, Lakota Nation
22 November 1993, Cry of the Earth

Speak Only the Truth

OUR FATHERS GAVE us many laws, which they had learned from their fathers. These laws were good. They told us to treat all people as they treated us; that we should never be the first to break a bargain; that it was a disgrace to tell a lie; that we should speak only the truth . . . . We were taught to believe that the Great Spirit sees and hears everything, and that he never forgets; that hereafter he will give every man a spirit-home according to his deserts . . .

CHIEF JOSEPH,
Nez Perce

The Great Law

THE GIVER OF LIFE – The Creator – did not intend that people abuse one another. Therefore, human societies must form governments that prevent the abuse of human beings by other human beings and ensure peace among nations and peoples.

Peace is the product of a society that strives to establish reason and righteousness.

'Righteousness' refers to the shared ideology of the people using their purest and most unselfish minds.

All people have a right to the things they need to survive – even those who do not or cannot work. No people or person has a right to deprive others of these things: food, clothing, shelter, and protection.

Human beings should use every effort to sit in council about, arbitrate, and negotiate their differences. Force should be resorted to only as a defence against the certain use of force.

Adapted from The Great Law of Peace
Haudenosaunee (Iroquois Six Nations)

Paying Attention

CENTRAL TO White Buffalo Woman's message, to all native spirituality, is the understanding that the Great Spirit lives in all things, enlivens all forms, and gives energy to all things in all realms of creation – including Earthly life . . .

. . . Ancient teachings call us to turn primary attention to the Sacred Web of Life, of which we are a part and with which we are so obviously entangled. This quality of attention – paying attention to the whole – is called among my people 'holiness'.

BROOKE MEDICINE EAGLE,
Crow

No Need for Setting Apart

WHENEVER, IN THE COURSE of the daily hunt the red hunter comes upon a scene that is strikingly beautiful or sublime – a black thundercloud with the rainbow's glowing arch above the mountain; a white waterfall in the heart of a green gorge; a vast prairie tinged with the blood-red of a sunset – he pauses for an instant in the attitude of worship. He sees no need for setting apart one day in seven as a holy day, since to him all days are God's.

OHIYESA (DR. CHARLES EASTMAN),
Santee Dakota

The Seventh Generation

IN OUR WAY OF LIFE . . . with every decision we make, we always keep in mind the Seventh Generation of children to come . . . . When we walk upon Mother Earth, we always plant our feet carefully, because we know that the faces of future generations are looking up at us from beneath the ground. We never forget them.

OREN LYONS,
Faithkeeper, Onondaga Nation
Earth Day 1993 Pledge

Tickling the Earth

WE ARE A matriarchal society. Even our language honours the women. It is a female language. When we dance, the men dance on the outside of the circle. The inside of the circle is to honor the women. When you dance to the ceremonial sounds of the Earth you are tickling Mother Earth, and giving her joy for all the things she gives us to stay alive.

KANARATITAKE (LORRAINE CANOE),
Mohawk

Giving Thanks

WHEN YOU ARISE in the morning,
give thanks for the morning light,
for your life and strength.
Give thanks for your food
and the joy of living.

If you see no reason for giving thanks,
the fault lies in yourself.

TECUMSEH,
Shawnee

You Will Know Each Other

IF YOU TALK TO the animals they will talk with you, and you will know each other. If you do not talk to them you will not know them, and what you do not know you will fear. What one fears, one destroys.

CHIEF DAN GEORGE,
Coast Salish

Experience Everything

To be a medicine man you have to experience everything, live life to the fullest. If you don't experience the human side of everything, how can you help teach or heal? To be a good medicine man, you've got to be humble. You've got to be lower than a worm and higher than an eagle.

ARCHIE FIRE LAME DEER,
Lakota
Gift of Power

Taste the Happiness of Giving

IT WAS OUR BELIEF that the love of possessions is a weakness to be overcome. Its appeal is to the material part, and if allowed its way, it will in time disturb one's spiritual balance. Therefore, children must early learn the beauty of generosity. They are taught to give what they prize most, that they may taste the happiness of giving.

OHIYESA (DR. CHARLES EASTMAN),
Santee Sioux

We Do Not Want Riches

LOOK AT ME — I am poor and naked, but I am the chief of the nation. We do not want riches, but we do want to train our children right. Riches would do us no good. We could not take them with us to the other world. We do not want riches. We want peace and love.

RED CLOUD,
Sioux

A Way to Give Back

THE MOST IMPORTANT thing to remember about ceremony is that it is a way for humans to give back to the Creation some of the energy that they are always receiving. The Earth Mother constantly gives us two-leggeds [human beings] a surface on which to place our two feet; Father Sun warms us, and Grandmother Moon brings dreams. The element of earth gives us a place to grow food and the ability to make homes and tools. The water keeps us alive. The fire warms our homes and cooks our food. The air gives us the sacred breath of life . . . . Through ceremony, we learn how to give back.

SUN BEAR,
Chippewa

The Cornerstone of Character

SILENCE IS THE absolute poise or balance of body, mind and spirit. The man who preserves his selfhood is ever calm and unshaken by the storms of existence . . . . If you ask him: 'What is silence?' he will answer: 'It is the Great Mystery. The Holy Silence is His voice.' If you ask: 'What are the fruits of silence?' he will say: 'They are self-control, true courage or endurance, patience, dignity and reverence. Silence is the cornerstone of character.'

OHIYESA (DR CHARLES EASTMAN),
Santee Sioux

Essence of Civilization

THE MAN WHO SAT on the ground in his tipi meditating on life and its meaning, accepting the kinship of all creatures and acknowledging unity with the universe of things, was infusing into his being the true essence of civilization. And when native man left off this form of development, his humanization was retarded in growth.

CHIEF LUTHER STANDING BEAR,
Oglala Sioux

Warriors of the Rainbow

THE INDIGENOUS TRIBES were not surprised when the black, white, and yellow peoples arrived on their shores, because their prophets had spoken of the coming of other races. They knew that the new tribes would overwhelm the ancient cultures of the land they called Turtle Island . . . . But it was said that in our times the spirit of the Indians would be born anew into all of the races that have gathered in this land. A portion of the different races of the rainbow colors will see that we are all one family. These Warriors of the Rainbow will bring with them a new time of living in harmony with our environment and with all peoples.

What Does It Matter?

THE COLOR OF THE SKIN makes no difference. What is good and just for one is good and just for the other, and the Great Spirit made all men brothers.

I have a red skin, but my grandfather was a white man. What does it matter? It is not the color of my skin that makes me good or bad.

WHITE SHIELD,
Arikara (Southern Cheyenne)

A Common Root

WE ARE ALL FLOWERS in the Great Spirit's garden. We share a common root, and the root is Mother Earth. The garden is beautiful because it has different colors in it, and those colors represent different traditions and cultural backgrounds.

GRANDFATHER DAVID MONONGYE,

Hopi

One Heart, One Mind

WE MUST STAND together, the four sacred colors of humanity, as the one family that we are, in the interest of peace. We must abolish nuclear and conventional weapons of war. We must raise leaders of peace. We must unite the religions of the world as a spiritual force strong enough to prevail in peace. We human beings are a spiritual energy that is thousands of times stronger than nuclear energy. Our energy is the combined will of all people with the spirit of the natural world, to be of one body, one heart, and one mind for peace.

LEON SHENANDOAH,
Tadadaho, Iroquois Six Nations
22 November 1993, Cry of the Earth

Four Questions

M Y GRANDFATHER Red Jacket
[Sagoyewatha] offered simple teachings.
For example, each person should ask himself or
herself four important questions that can serve as
guides: Am I happy in what I'm doing? Is what
I'm doing going to add to the confusion in the
world? What am I doing to bring about peace
and contentment? And how will I be
remembered when I am gone.

YEHWENODE (TWYLAH NITSCH),
Seneca Nation

What is Life?

WHAT IS LIFE? It is the flash of a firefly in the night. It is the breath of a buffalo in the winter time. It is the little shadow which runs across the grass and loses itself in the Sunset.

CROWFOOT,

Blackfoot, 1890, on his deathbed

After All This, The Great Mystery

AFTER ALL THE GREAT religions have been preached and expounded, or have been revealed by brilliant scholars, or have been written in fine books and embellished in fine language with finer covers, man – all man – is still confronted with The Great Mystery.

CHIEF LUTHER STANDING BEAR,
Oglala Sioux

Something We Must Have

LOVE IS SOMETHING you and I must have.
We must have it because our spirit feeds
upon it. We must have it because without it we
become weak and faint. Without love our self-
esteem weakens. Without it our courage fails.
Without love we can no longer look
confidently at the world. We turn inward and
begin to feed upon our own personalities, and
little by little we destroy it ourselves.

With it we are creative. With it we march
tirelessly. With it, and with it alone, we are able
to sacrifice for others.

CHIEF DAN GEORGE,
Coast Salish

The Sacred Web

THE PEOPLE WHO are living on this planet
need to break with the narrow concept of
human liberation, and begin to see liberation as
something that needs to be extended to the
whole of the Natural World. What is needed is
the liberation of all things that support life – the
air, the waters, the trees – all the things which
support the sacred web of life.

A Basic Call to Consciousness,
Haudenosaunee Address
to the Western World,
(1977)

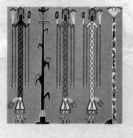

Consider This Matter Seriously

WE ARE NOW living in the fourth and final world of the Hopi. We are at a most critical time in human history. It is a crossroads at which the outcome of our actions will decide the fate of all life on earth . . . . This is the last world, we are not going anywhere from here. If we destroy this, the highest world, which is like heaven, we will be given no other chances . . . . Let us consider this matter seriously so that this world is not destroyed, so that we can continue to live and save this land and life for the generations to come.

MARTIN GASHWESEOMA,
Caretaker, Hopi Nation
22 November 1993, Cry of the Earth

The Eastern Door

JUST THIS YEAR [1993] the opening of the Eastern Door took place in Cape Spear, Newfoundland, Canada, the furthest eastern point in North America. The circle of the Medicine Wheel is now complete. The Wabanaki [People of the Light] have joined the circle under the following philosophy: 'Heal you the self – you help to heal the family, the family helps to heal the community, the community helps to heal the nation, the nations help to heal the world. It is time for us all to stop blaming one another, heal from our wounds, and move forward – for the survival of the world as we know it is in our hands.

DAVID GEHUE,
Spiritual Counselor, Mic Mac Nation
22 November 1993, Cry of the Earth

Lead a Simple Life

THE GREAT SPIRIT based us here to take care of this land and life for Him through prayer, meditations, ceremonies, and rituals, and to lead a simple life close to the Earth. That's what we have been doing. Governments talk all the time about human rights, equality, justice, and all those things, but they have never done anything for the native people. Never . . . . So it's time that they do that – live up to their talk – otherwise nature is going to take over. Earthquakes, flooding, destruction by volcanic eruptions, tidal waves, things like that . . . . It's already happening, and it takes that kind of thing to wake up many people who are controlling this land by money and power and just ripping everything from the Earth. They are doing something that is not right in the law of the Great Spirit and the law of nature.

THOMAS BANYACYA,
Hopi Elder
22 November 1993, Cry of the Earth

Remember the Key

I N THESE TIMES of turmoil, every human being is being asked to remember their connection to the Creator and to the Earth Mother, making those connections strong. Each person's connection to the Great Mystery, to the Earth Mother, to the spirits of the Ancestors and to their Spiritual Essences holds the key to finding the balance . . . . Human beings tend to forget that no man-made organization is the Source, the only Source is the Great Mystery, the Creator. Every human being must answer to that Source, not to another human being.

JAMIE SAMS,
Choctaw and Iroquois

Path to Survival

BROTHERS AND SISTERS: We bring to
your thought and minds that right-minded
human beings seek to promote above all else the
life of all things. We direct to your minds that
peace is not merely the absence of war, but the
constant effort to maintain harmonious existence
between all peoples, from individual to
individual, and between humans and the other
beings of this planet. We point out to you that a
Spiritual Consciousness is the Path to Survival of
Humankind.

The Haudenosaunee Declaration, 1979

ABOUT THE AUTHOR

Steven McFadden is the author of several books, including two full-length works on contemporary Native American themes: Profiles in Wisdom: Native Elders Speak About the Earth (Bear & Co., 1991) and Ancient Voices, Current Affairs: The Legend of the Rainbow Warriors (Bear & Co., 1992).

He is Director of The Wisdom Conservancy at Merriam Hill Education Center, a private, non-profit, non-sectarian institute. With the support of its members and staff, The Wisdom Conservancy uses modern media to conserve, communicate, and encourage wisdom in all world cultures.

For information contact:

The Wisdom Conservancy
at Merriam Hill Education Center
148 Merriam Hill
Greenville, NH 03048 USA

ACKNOWLEDGEMENTS

The publishers would like to thank the following for
permission to reproduce their illustrations:
Fortean Picture Library – pages 10-11. 18. 32
Mary Evans Picture Library – page 34
Museum of Navajo Ceremonial Art – page 40
Peter Newark's Western Americana – pages 8-9. 30. 46